Tandi's Brave Friends and Special Helpers

Real Life Stories of Kids and their Dissociative Experiences

Michele M. Yarberry

To order additional copies of this book, contact:
Xlibris
844-714-8691
www.Xlibris.com
Orders@Xlibris.com

Library of Congress Control Number: 2022920973
ISBN: Softcover   978-1-6698-5533-0
        Hardcover   978-1-6698-5534-7
        EBook   978-1-6698-5532-3

Print information available on the last page

Rev. date: 01/16/2022

Tandi's Brave Friends and Special Helpers

Real Life Stories of Kids and their Dissociative Experiences

by Michele M. Yarberry, LPC, NCC, RPT, CBCP

Illustrations by Andreea Hompoth-Voicu

INTRODUCTION

Dear Parents, Caregivers, and Professionals:

Thank you for your interest in my book. My intentions and hopes are:

1. That this book will bring you, the adults, a better understanding of the internal experiences of some children who have experienced various traumatic events and how it has affected their behaviors.

2. For the children, to help normalize their internal experiences as a result of experiencing traumatic events and to know that they are not alone.

3. To guide parents, caregivers, and professionals in obtaining more information, support, and effective treatment options through the free resources that are provided on the resource pages.

The over-lapping presenting symptoms/behaviors of Complex Trauma, Dissociation, and Complex PTSD with those of other disorders often lead to a misdiagnosis or missed diagnosis. Complex Trauma and Dissociation are not always included in trauma assessments. Children may present with physical symptoms, such as numbness, pain, aches and/or body parts feeling disconnected. Other children may report parts of self, characters, animals, etc. that live inside their heads and/or bodies, which affect their behaviors.

According to the International Society for the Study of Trauma & Dissociation (ISSTD) definition, as described in their *ISSTD Fact Sheet for Caregivers*:

> "Dissociation can be considered a biological and psychological response that may occur during or after traumatic events as a means of coping. Dissociation is when the brain disconnects awareness from experience, feeling, sensation, and/or the self. Children, like adults, may dissociate when they are overwhelmed by fear or pain and cannot escape. When there is no escape from the widespread and repetitive nature of complex trauma, children may use dissociation to disconnect from and block out what is happening to them, what they are feeling, what they are thinking, who is causing the harm or pain, and what they are sensing in order to cope and survive. The ability to dissociate is rooted in protection and the innate ability to survive the unimaginable.
>
> A child may dissociate during and after any of the traumatic events listed above, or when reminded about any of the events listed above, even long after the event(s) are over. Reminders are called "triggers." It is important to remember that if your child receives support and feels safe soon after a frightening event, any dissociation may be temporary and, therefore, not problematic. Besides dissociating during and after a traumatic event, for some people dissociation can become a longer-term coping strategy to get through stressful, but potentially not traumatic, situations in everyday life".

Please feel free to send your and/or your child's feedback/responses to me at tandi@ liberatedlivingforyou.com!

Sincerely,
Michele M. Yarberry, LPC, NCC, RPT, CBCP

In the following stories, Tandi is a fictional character. Pseudo names were used for the featured children. Permission was granted by all clients and parents for use in this book.

Hello, my name is Tandi and I am excited for you to meet my brave friends and their very special helpers! These very special helpers protected my brave friends during and after the bigger than kid-sized things that happened to them. Bigger than kidsized things are super scary things that cause kids to feel like they might die, cannot get away or might get really hurt.

Thankfully, kids have really smart brains, minds, and bodies that work together to create special helpers who live in their heads and bodies. These special helpers gave my friends power to help them survive and thrive. Survive means they lived; thrive means they kept growing, learning, and becoming amazing kids. Because my brave friends sur-thrived the bigger than kid-size things, they are *surthrivors*!

You will hear a little about the power, strength, and super energy their special helpers gave them when they were scared. You might be hearing new words like adopted, adoptive, orphanage, and Play Therapist. Sometimes, birth parents cannot take care of their babies and take them to an orphanage. An orphanage is a place where children and babies are cared for until they are joined with parents who very much want a baby or child. This is called adoption and the adopted child becomes part of the family, known as an adoptive family. A Play Therapist is someone who understands the special helpers' roles and how to work with them and the very brave surthrivors.

Are you ready to meet my brave friends and their special helpers?

Terrific, let's go!

Please meet my friend, Jordan, an active 6-year-old, who likes to play sports. She, also, enjoys camping and fishing with her family. When Jordan was a baby, she was very sick and some of the helpers were created when this bigger than kid-size thing happened! Some of her family members died when she was a young child, which was another bigger than kid-size thing. Other special helpers came to help Jordan with her sad, scared, and confused feelings.

Some of Jordan's special helpers have younger brothers and sisters, just like she does. The fairies are older and very wise. Sad Jordan held onto the sad feelings for Jordan, so she did not have to feel them. Bad Jordan would try to hit the doctors and her parents, because she thought that Jordan needed to be kept away from them. Jordan's mom, dad, and doctors did not know any of Jordan's special helpers or they would have helped them, too, when the very scary things happened. Jordan's parents learned how to take care of Jordan's helpers and Bad Jordan learned she could do good things, so she changed her name to Good Jordan! Other helpers learned how to use their energy and strength to help Jordan know that her parents and doctors were helping her.

Please meet my 7-year-old friend, Jason, a very clever boy who likes to read, play sports, and spend time with his best friend. Jason was very sick, when he was born. His mom and dad had to take him to the hospital often. Sometimes, his parents helped the doctors give Jason medicine. He was scared, confused, and cried a lot when he had to go see the doctors. This was a bigger than kid-size thing that kept happening for a long time.

Some of Jason's special helpers were animals, insects, older kids, and one who was a baby. A very special scorpion helper gave Jason strength to scream at the doctors and his parents, because the scorpion thought that would keep Jason safe. The very young special helper, thought Jason was still a baby and would cry a lot when something happened that reminded him of the bigger than kid-size thing. This confused Jason, because it made Jason cry, too and he was not always sure why!

In time, the baby learned that Jason was 7 years old and no longer sick so, he did not need to cry or be scared. The strong scorpion learned that Jason was safe, healthy, and no longer needed hospital visits. The scorpion also learned that doctors and parents had not been mean to Jason. The scorpion was able to understand that everyone had done their best to help Jason get well. After Jason's parents learned about what was happening on the inside, they understood how to better help Jason and his special helpers, too.

Please meet my 3-year-old friend, Derrick. He loves to draw, play with his baby sister, and help his parents with chores around the house. His birth mommy and daddy were very young when he was born. They did not know how to take care of baby Derrick. Sometimes, they left him with other people that Derrick did not know. Derrick did not feel safe and was confused because some of the other people did not know when to feed him or change his diapers. Derrick was hungry and uncomfortable a lot of the time. This was a bigger than kid-size thing and he needed his special helpers to sur-thrive. When Derrick's grandparents learned what had happened, they brought him into their home and took care of him. Soon he was adopted by his new mom and dad, who were very excited to welcome baby Derrick into their family.

As Derrick learned to walk and talk, he also screamed, cried a lot, and sometimes hit other people. He was very angry, especially with his mom. Derrick's parents were confused and did not know that a bulldozer, baby, and a big spider were some of the special helpers that lived inside of Derrick's head. The special helpers did not know that Derrick's adoptive parents were their parents, too. They did not trust Derrick's new parents and thought they needed to protect him. With the help of a Play Therapist, Derrick's parents learned how to show his special helpers that they and Derrick were safe and loved.

Please meet my friend, Mukisa, who is 10 years old and loves to play sports. Mukisa was adopted from a country in Africa. His birth mother was not able to give Mukisa the care that he needed and he did not always get enough food. He lived with his aunt for a while, but she also could not provide him with a safe home. Mukisa's aunt thought it would be best to take him to a church. She left him there, and did not return. Thankfully, there was a kind man at the church who found an orphanage, where Mukisa was given food, shelter, and clothing.

Mukisa felt scared, alone, and confused, because did not have his family and did not know where they were. This was a very sad and bigger than kid-size thing for Mukisa. Some of his special helpers on the inside were very angry about what had happened to him.

His adoptive family was confused about Mukisa's behaviors. They did everything they could to give him a good home. But, he cried a lot. One of his special helpers remembered when he did not have enough food to eat, which caused him to steal and hide food. Other helpers would keep Mukisa awake at night, because they were curious and wanted to explore places. These helpers also took things that belonged to other people, which caused big problems. His parents took him to see a Play Therapist who understood what was going on inside of Mukisa.

After his family learned about his special helpers, they understood more about what was going on inside and outside. When Mukisa, forgot about things that happened or when he stole things from people or cried or became angry, his family made sense of his behaviors. His parents became very good at working with Mukisa and his special helpers. His special helpers were insects, animals, and people, who learned to work together as a team to make life better.

Please meet my 3-year-old friend, Wayne, who was also adopted from an African country. Wayne's birth mommy and daddy could not take care of him when he was born. Baby Wayne lived in an orphanage where people cared for his needs the best they could. Wayne had food, clothes, and a bed, but he did not have a mommy and daddy to give him the love that he needed. This was a bigger than kid-size thing and his special helpers knew just how to help him during this time.

Wayne's adoptive mommy and daddy were excited to bring baby Wayne home. He even had an older brother to play with and got to do a lot of fun things. Wayne's new family loved him very much! As Wayne got a little older, he would get angry and sometimes hit his mommy, daddy, and brother. He got frustrated because he did not learn to talk like other kids his age and he often cried when he did not get his way. Wayne had trouble following directions at preschool and getting along with other children in his class. His mommy and daddy were very smart and knew they needed more help.

Wayne's parents found a Play Therapist who taught them about special helpers that lived on the inside. They better understood his behaviors and could better help Wayne. His special helper was a baby. In time, the baby realized that Wayne was 3 years old, safe, and loved by his family. Wayne was then able to get along with his friends and did not always get mad, when he did not get his way.

Please meet my friend, Sadie, who is 5 years old and was born in China. She is very creative and loves doing artwork, especially if glitter is included. Sadie's birth mommy could not care for her and she was taken to an orphanage. Sadie is deaf, so she could not hear and did not learn a language or know how to communicate with her caregivers. This was a bigger than kid-size thing and she needed special helpers for this.

Her special helpers were little girls and one was a baby. They gave her strength during really hard times in the orphanage. One day, a wonderful family traveled to China to adopt Sadie, when she was three years old. But this was so scary for her because Sadie had only seen and known people that were from China. All of her caregivers had been Chinese women. Sadie could not talk or hear what the very different-looking people were saying to her. She did not understand why she was leaving the orphanage. Sadie cried and screamed a lot for a long time because she was so afraid. Her special helpers thought she needed protection and caused Sadie to hit her adoptive brothers and parents. It was very difficult for her family, too, and they did not know how to help Sadie feel better; however, they knew American Sign Language and taught her how to talk with her hands. Sadie learned the language quite easily, but she still cried, screamed, and did things she was not allowed to do.

Her mom found a Play Therapist who knew American Sign Language and had a therapy dog that knew some hand signals. Sadie was excited that she could communicate with the dog using her hands and make him do tricks! Sadie described her special helpers using Oriental nesting dolls and told her therapist which ones got mad at her mom. This helped her mom understand Sadie's anger and that the special helpers thought this would keep her safe. Sadie and her special helpers learned that her adoptive mother and family would love and care for all of them. The special helpers also learned better ways of expressing their big feelings.

I hope that you enjoyed meeting my friends and learning about their stories. Please join me in my next book to hear about the things that helped Sadie and her special helpers join together.

See you soon!

Resources

Child Dissociative Checklist: https://www.ce-credit.com/articles/102019/Session_2_Provided-Articles-1of2.pdf

ISSTD Fact Sheet for Caregivers. https://www.isst-d.org/wp-content/uploads/2022/04/CA-Caregivers-Fact-Sheet-1.pdf

Professional Non-member Resources: https://www.isst-d.org/resources/

Public Resources: https://www.isst-d.org/public-resources-home/

Silberg, J. (2022) 2nd Edition. The child survivor. New York: Routledge

Waters, F. S. (2016). Healing the fractured child: diagnosis and treatment of youth with dissociation. New York: Springer Publishing Company.

Michele's Articles

Yarberry, M. (2022) https://news.isst-d.org/a-multi-modal-integrative-approach-in-treatment-of-children-with-complex-trauma-dissociation/. ISSTD News, Clinical Reflections Column

Yarberry, M. (2021) https://news.isst-d.org/the-flash-technique-for-dissociative-children/. ISSTD News, Kid's Korner

Yarberry M. (2019). https://news.isst-d.org/proposal-to-the-field-fourth-phase-in-treatment-of-dissociation-protocol/. ISSTD News, Kid's Korner

Yarberry, M. (2018) https://news.isst-d.org/squaks-nuzzles-tail-wags-woofs-and-whinnies-an-experiential-glimpse-into-animalequine-assisted-psychotherapyplay-therapy/. ISSTD News, Kid's Korner

Printed in the United States
by Baker & Taylor Publisher Services